Play it Cool

Flute

James Rae

Ten easy pieces for flute and piano

UNIVERSAL EDITION

ISMN M-008-06495-1 ISBN 3-7024-0853-3 UPC 8-03452-00619-0

Play it Cool

Designed for the beginner, this collection of pieces provides stimulating performance material in various styles at the easiest possible level. The accompaniments (piano or CD) provide a good solid backing and will inspire the soloist to play with energy and enthusiasm. I have made much deliberate use of the repetition of phrases, as I feel that this is the best way for pupils to absorb new rhythms. This approach, together with the strong support given by the accompaniments, will develop confidence, which is an essential aspect of any musical performance.

Not only is *Play it Cool* suitable for group tuition, it is, in addition, ideal as elementary ensemble material as these ten pieces are also available for other instruments.

James Rae

Contents and Track List

Each piece is fully recorded with a professional soloist for listening and learning.
The track following provides the accompaniment minus the solo for playing along.

 **Track 2/3**

Rum Point

*This piece requires a very solid pulse. Count all your note-lengths
very carefully and don't be tempted to rush. Keep it steady!*

JAMES RAE

Solid 'reggae' feel ♩ = 96

Printed in England
All Rights Reserved

UE 21 101 L

Track 4/5 **Lazy Cat Blues**

*This piece is a typical example of a slow 12 bar blues. Play it with a totally 'laid back'
feel and watch your counting on the tied quaver/minim rhythms. Really take your
time with this one and don't be tempted to speed up. The slower, the better!*

JAMES RAE

4

Track 6/7 # Wimbledon Waltz

Play this piece as smoothly as possible with no sharp edges. Aim for nice long phrases and always count the dotted minims accurately.

JAMES RAE

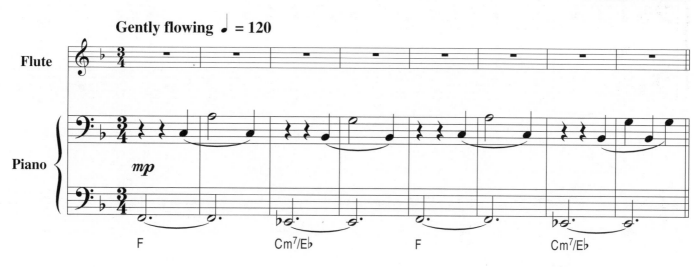

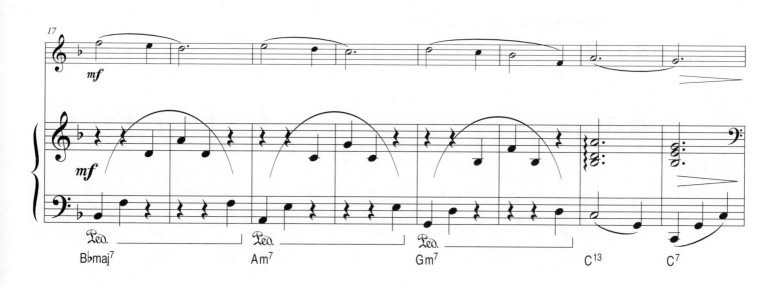

6

 Track 8/9 # Hard Graft

*Always maintain a solid beat throughout this piece and try to
achieve a sense of building towards a climax at bar 20.*

JAMES RAE

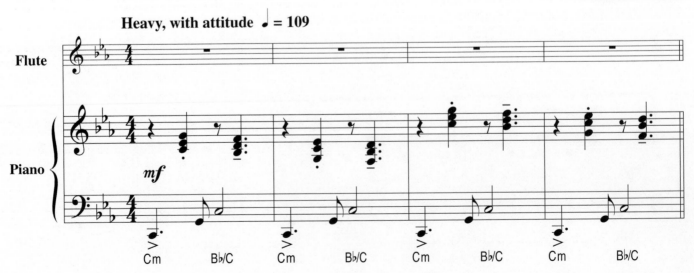

UE 21 101 L

Track 10/11

The Guv'nor

*Lots of controlled power required here! Observe all the articulation carefully
and always play the accents strongly, as if you really mean business!*

JAMES RAE

Track 12/13

Curtain Up!

*This piece is typical of a theatrical opening number. Feel the strong two beats
in a bar – not four. Aim for a sense of lively excitement throughout.*

JAMES RAE

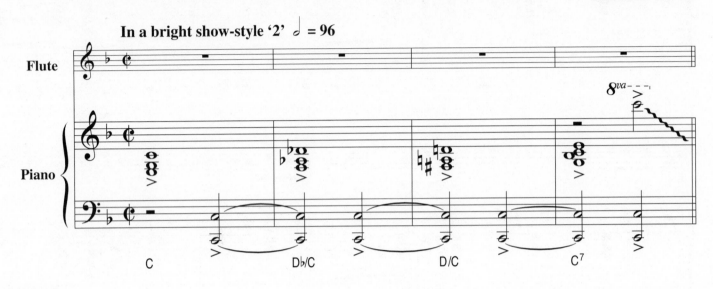

Flute

Play it Cool

James Rae

Track 2/3   # Rum Point

*This piece requires a very solid pulse. Count all your note-lengths
very carefully and don't be tempted to rush. Keep it steady!*

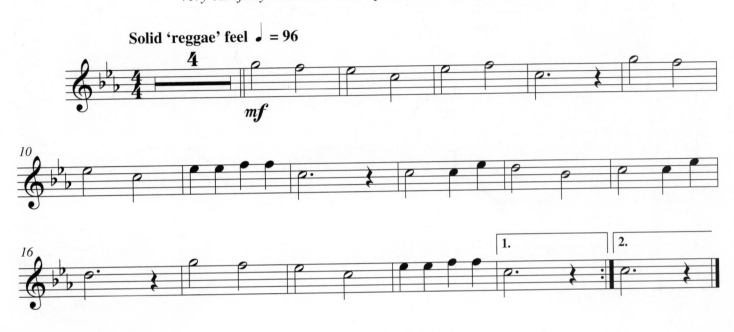

Track 4/5   # Lazy Cat Blues ✓

*This piece is a typical example of a slow 12 bar blues. Play it with a totally 'laid back'
feel and watch your counting on the tied quaver/minim rhythms. Really take your
time with this one and don't be tempted to speed up. The slower, the better!*

2

 **Track 6/7** # Wimbledon Waltz

Play this piece as smoothly as possible with no sharp edges. Aim for
nice long phrases and always count the dotted minims accurately.

 **Track 8/9** # Hard Graft

Always maintain a solid beat throughout this piece and try to
achieve a sense of building towards a climax at bar 20.

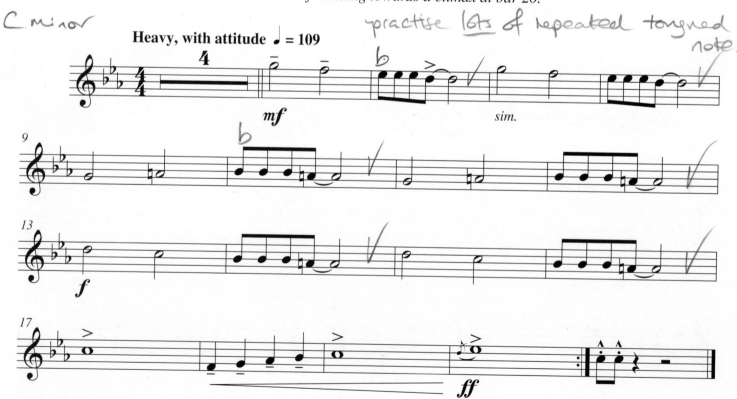

UE 21 101a L

Track 10/11

The Guv'nor

*Lots of controlled power required here! Observe all the articulation carefully
and always play the accents strongly, as if you really mean business!*

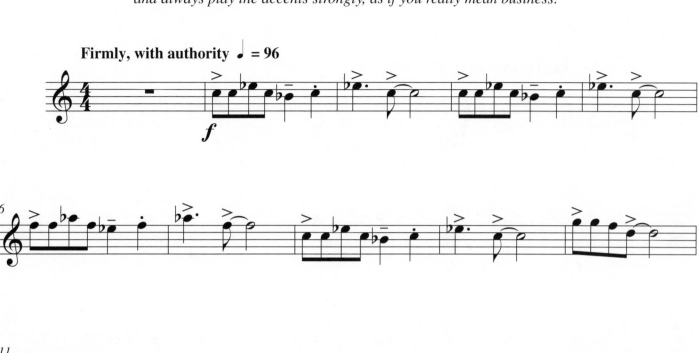

UE 21 101a L

Track 12/13

Curtain Up!

*This piece is typical of a theatrical opening number. Feel the strong two beats
in a bar – not four. Aim for a sense of lively excitement throughout.*

Bruno's Tune

The essence of 'funk' music is in its powerful driving energy which is usually the result of placing a solid melody over an intricate rhythmic accompaniment. Always maintain a firm pulse when you play this piece so that your melody can fit neatly over the backing.

UE 21 101a L

6

Rumba

*The Rumba is a Latin American Dance with the same repeated
rhythmic accompaniment in each bar. Pay special attention to the
slurs and always count the dotted minim lengths accurately.*

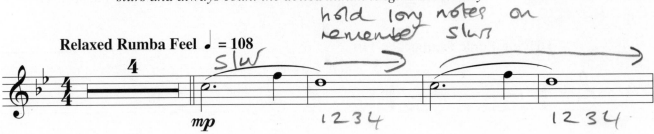

UE 21 101a L

Gate 24

Cool is the name of the game here. Aim to play in long, smooth phrases observing all slurs carefully. Pay particular attention to the accidentals in the section from bars 21 to 33.

8

Blowin' Cool

8 *Really let your hair down and 'roll in the dirt' with this one! Pay special attention to the section from bar 15 where the accompaniment cuts out and you are left high and dry. Always keep the quavers swinging.*

803 UE 21 101a L

8 LI/02

Track 14/15 # Bruno's Tune

The essence of 'funk' music is in its powerful driving energy which is usually the result of placing a solid melody over an intricate rhythmic accompaniment. Always maintain a firm pulse when you play this piece so that your melody can fit neatly over the backing.

JAMES RAE

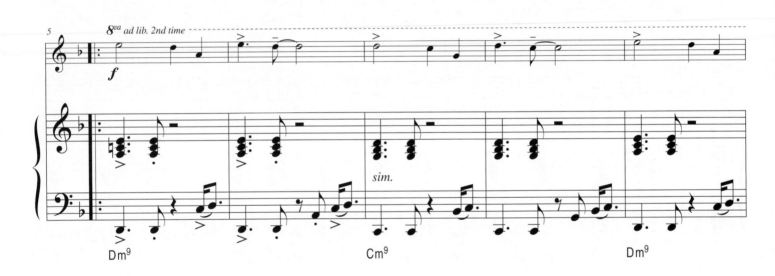

UE 21 101 L

UE 21 101 L

13

14

Track 16/17

Rumba

The Rumba is a Latin American Dance with the same repeated rhythmic accompaniment in each bar. Pay special attention to the slurs and always count the dotted minim lengths accurately.

JAMES RAE

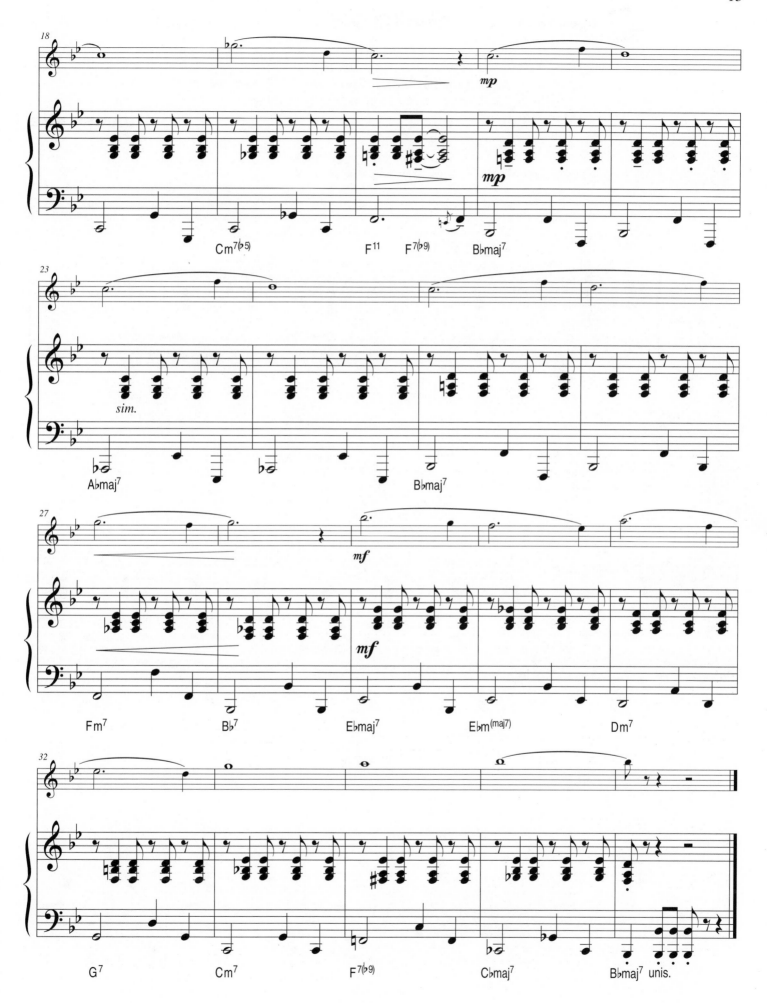

Track 18/19

Gate 24

Cool is the name of the game here. Aim to play in long, smooth
phrases observing all slurs carefully. Pay particular attention
to the accidentals in the section from bars 21 to 33.

JAMES RAE

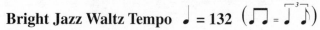

Bright Jazz Waltz Tempo ♩ = 132

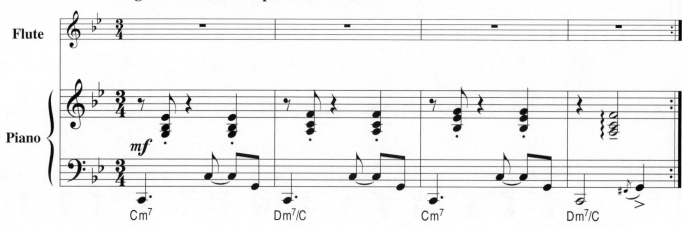

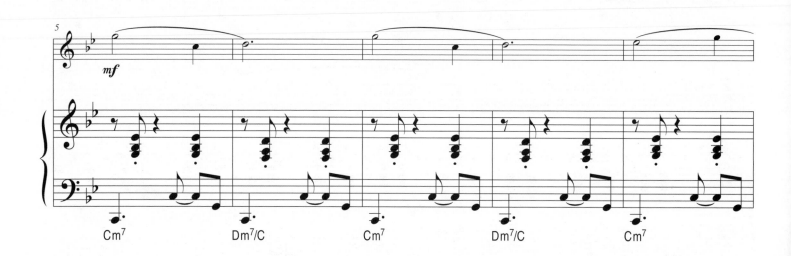

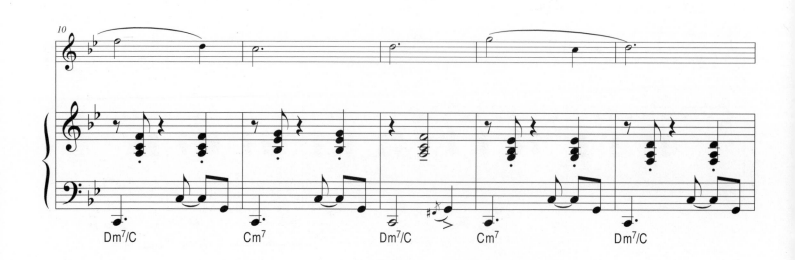

18

UE 21 101 L

 **Track 20/21**

Blowin' Cool

Really let your hair down and 'roll in the dirt' with this one! Pay special attention to the section from bar 15 where the accompaniment cuts out and you are left high and dry. Always keep the quavers swinging.

JAMES RAE

UE 21 101 L

EASY JAZZY
WOODWIND

For early ventures into the syncopated patterns of jazz

Solo with piano

EASY JAZZY FLUTE *James Rae*
UE 16 581

EASY JAZZY CLARINET *Paul Harvey*
UE 19 214

EASY JAZZY SAXOPHONE *James Rae*
UE 16 578

Duets

EASY JAZZY DUETS – FLUTES *James Rae*
UE 16 587

EASY JAZZY DUETS – CLARINETS *James Rae*
UE 16 552

EASY JAZZY DUETS – SAXOPHONES *James Rae*
UE 16 551

EASY JAZZY DUETS – FLUTE & CLARINET *James Rae*
UE 16 588

EASY JAZZY DUETS – RECORDERS *Brian Bonsor*
UE 16 586

UE
Universal Edition